Why You Should Not Have Sex Before Marriage

Why You Should Not Have Sex Before Marriage
The Christian Perspective

SAM GOODE

The Hermit Kingdom Press
Cheltenham ♦ Seoul ♦ Bangalore ♦ Cebu

WHY YOU SHOULD NOT HAVE SEX BEFORE MARRIAGE: THE CHRISTIAN PERSPECTIVE

Copyright © 2006 by Sam Goode

All rights reserved. No part of this book may be reproduced in any form or by any means, electronic or mechanical, including photocopying, recording, or by any information storage and retrieval system (including all forms of computer files), without permission in writing from the publisher.

ISBN 1-59689-061-4 (paperback)
ISBN 1-59689-062-2 (ebook)

Write-To Address:

The Hermit Kingdom Press
12325 Imperial Highway, Suite 156
Norwalk, California 90650
United States of America

Hermit Kingdom
12 South Bridge, Suite 370
Edinburgh, EH1 1DD
Scotland

Library of Congress Cataloging-in-Publication Data

Goode, Sam.
  Why you should not have sex before marriage : the Christian perspective / Sam Goode.
    p. cm.
  ISBN 1-59689-061-4 (pbk. : alk. paper)
  1. Sex--Religious aspects--Christianity. 2. Chastity. 3. Sexual abstinence--Religious aspects--Christianity. 4. Marriage--Religious aspects--Christianity. 5. Sexual ethics. I. Title.
  BT708.G655 2006
  241'.66--dc22
                                                    2006017179

For all teenage Christians around the world

Contents

Introduction 1

Bible's Teaching 9

For Yourself 25

For Your Future Life Partner 53

For Christ's Church 81

Conclusion 101

"Courage is contagious.
When a brave man takes a stand,
the spines of others are often stiffened."

Rev. Billy Graham

Introduction

Introduction

The greatest temptation facing a teenage Christian is to have premarital sex. This should not surprise anyone. Sex is everywhere. It is as if there are "sex pushers" who are legitimized by society.

Hollywood seems to play the biggest role in "telling" Christian teenagers that they are missing out if they are not having sex. That like animals, having sex with anyone "you feel like it" is a good thing. Movies coming out of Hollywood often seem to take an aggressive stance against the teaching of the Bible. Hollywood often tries to tell Christian teenagers that it is "natural" or "normal" to have premarital sex. Is Hollywood God?

The music industry often encourages premarital sex by making it seem like a hip thing. The cool people have premarital sex, so if you don't have premarital sex, then you are not cool. The marketing of "cool" is often equated with marketing of premarital sex. Should the secular music Industry play an agent for the Devil and his desire to knock Christian teenagers down?

Teenage magazines also have a hand as a "pusher" of premarital sex. Many teenage magazines assume that teenagers should have premarital sex and often the articles reflect this assumption. Christian teenagers reading secular teenage magazines may be compelled to question themselves and their place in the American society. Teenage magazines, thus, play a type of *yellow journalism* of propaganda against the teachings of the Bible. Should teenage magazines become a powerful ad for premarital sex and bring about the moral downfall of Christian teenagers?

Unfortunately, it is not only secular agencies and media that "push" premarital sex. There are even so-called "Christian leaders" who legitimate pre-marital sex. Against the teaching of the 10 Commandments and against the instruction of the New Testament, some people who teach Christian teenagers wrongly tell them that premarital sex is okay. Should these false prophets warned about in the book of Jeremiah in the Old Testament continue to teach that premarital sex is okay and corrupt Christian churches in America?

Even without all these "pushers" of premarital sex, Christian teenagers face temptations to give in to premarital sex. Biologically, teenagers have raging hormones. Strong hormones cause teenagers to desire sex physically. Emotionally, too, hormones have their effect on teenagers. Christian teenagers are not immune to hormonal changes and their impact. The temptation for premarital sex is very real, physically.

There is also the curiosity factor. Not having had sexual experiences, Christian teenagers often find themselves curious about sex and sexual experiences. Curiosity often compels Christian teenagers to the brink of giving into premarital sex. Indeed, curiosity coupled with strong hormones often becomes an overpowering force in tempting Christian teenagers to commit the offense against God by engaging in premarital sex.

It is very difficult in America today to discourage Christian teenagers to stay pure in Christ by not engaging in premarital sex. All the odds are stacked against maintaining purity.

Introduction

It is precisely because it is so difficult to fight the forces of Satan that we must not give up our struggle against them. Christians must not lay down arms and play dead. Christians must not give up and let the Enemy have his way with us. Christians must rise to the challenge. Christians must find ways to uphold the teachings of the Bible. Christian teenagers must figure out how they can beat this evil force against the teachings of the Bible.

First place to start, of course, is the Bible. It is important to turn to the Bible to understand Bible's teachings against premarital sex and instructions regarding sexual purity. Christian teenagers must arm themselves with spiritual weapons to counter the assault against the teachings of the Bible. Christian teenagers must know, understand, and apply the teachings of the Bible in their lives. Furthermore, Christian teenagers should be able to throw some counter-attack against the forces of Satan to "push" premarital sex on society.

Having the Bible as the ultimate standard, Christian teenagers should use the brain that God has given them to find creative ways to engage in the spiritual warfare. Like any warfare, spiritual warfare requires strategy, appropriate application of spiritual arms and weapons to bring about the spiritual advance, to knock down of enemy forces and strategies. Christian teenagers can step up to the plate and win battles for Jesus Christ, who is Savior LORD and God.

In fact, Christian teenagers can prove to be the greatest Christian warriors to fight the forces of Satan "pushing" premarital sex. Christian teenagers can play the valiant and proud role of Christian soldiers crusading against anti-Bible forces in the American society and purifying the American society for Jesus Christ, who is the King of kings and the LORD of lords.

It is in this spirit that this book is written – to raise up Christian warriors among Christian teenagers to fight the forces of Satan which try to tempt Christian teenagers to commit the serious offense against God by engaging in premarital sex.

Bible's Teaching

Bible's Teaching

The Bible's teaching is clear. Premarital sex offends God. This is the principle found in the Old Testament as well as in the New Testament. Historically, the Christian Church has upheld this principle for over 2000 years.

In order to understand the Bible's prohibition of premarital sex, it is important to examine the Bible's warning against sexual immorality.

In the Old Testament, there are numerous injunctions against sexual impurity. When we look at Leviticus 18, we see how seriously God considers sexual immorality. In fact God sets specific regulation against sexual immorality. Leviticus 18:6-18 commands:

> *Do not dishonor your father by having sexual relations with your mother. She is your mother; do not have relations with her. Do not have sexual relations with your father's wife; that would dishonor your father. Do not have sexual relations with your sister, either your father's daughter or your mother's daughter, whether she was born in the same home or elsewhere. Do not have sexual relations with your son's daughter or your daughter's daughter; that would dishonor you. Do not have sexual relations with the daughter of your father's wife, born to your father; she is your sister. Do not have sexual relations with your*

> *father's sister; she is your father's close relative. Do not have sexual relations with your mother's sister, because she is your mother's close relative. Do not dishonor your father's brother by approaching his wife to have sexual relations; she is your aunt. Do not have sexual relations with your daughter-in-law. She is your son's wife; do not have relations with her. Do not have sexual relations with both a woman and her daughter. Do not have sexual relations with either her son's daughter or her daughter's daughter; they are her close relative. That is wickedness. Do not take your wife's sister as a rival wife and have sexual relations with her while your wife is living.*

It is clear that Leviticus 18 testifies to the seriousness of sexual purity. God is so concerned with sexual purity, the Bible describes in specific details with whom you are not allowed to have sex.

One can easily see that Hollywood movies stand against this emphatic prohibition of sex with relatives that is found in the Bible. Hollywood implicitly supports the idea that sex prohibited by the Bible is okay. Thus, Hollywood becomes an "enabler" of illicit sex – sex that is illegal under God's Law.

The Bible teaches that having sex with a close relative is sexual impurity. Besides teaching with whom you are not allowed to have sex, the Old Testament also teaches what kind of sex you are not supposed to have.

The Bible is emphatic in condemning homosexuality – sex between the same sex (whether it is between a man and a man or between a woman and a woman). Leviticus 18:22 teaches: *"Do not lie with a man as one lies with a woman; that is detestable."*

The Bible is clear about the seriousness of homosexuality as a crime punishable under God's Law. This is evident in Genesis 19.

In Genesis 19:1, we see two angels visiting Sodom in the evening. It becomes clear in the context of the whole chapter that they are there to give witness to the wickedness of the city, for which God committed genocide against the people of Sodom and Gomorrah as divine punishment.

Genesis 19:2-3 shows Abraham's nephew Lot persuading the two angels to come to his house for a meal. The problem starts after the two heavenly guests have their meal.

In Genesis 19:4, we see that *"all the men from every part of the city of Sodom – both young and old"* surrounding the house. Their purpose for the gathering was in order to homosexual rape the two angels who appeared before them in human form. The men of Sodom cry out: *"Where are the men who came to you tonight? Bring them out to us so that we can have sex with them."* The homosexual men of the city did not mince words and made their intentions very clear.

When Lot tries to intervene on behalf of the angels, the gay men of the city kept pressuring Lot to help them rape the two angels who appeared in human form. In Genesis 19:9, we see the gay men of the city trying to break down the door in order to drag the angels out to homosexual rape them.

The episode has a happy ending in that the angels pulled Lot back into the house to safety. They then made the gay men blind, so they could not find the door. There was not going to be homosexual rape that night.

The episode in Genesis 19 was meant to show why God decided to annihilate the people of Sodom and Gomorrah. They were seeped in homosexuality and in approving homosexuality. The city became so corrupt in God's eyes that homosexuality was not only normal, homosexual rape became a visible reality with the participation of many in the city.

This should put up red flags in the minds of Americans. Hollywood movies often portray homosexuality as normal and not out of the ordinary. In other words, Hollywood tries to normalize the perception of homosexuals in the American society.

Just think of the last Hollywood movie that you have seen. Were there gay individuals in the movie? Were they portrayed in a positive light? As normal people?

The answers to these questions probably will be "yes." Hollywood is going against the teachings of the Bible and is opposing God's Law with shamelessness. Hollywood is, therefore, an "enabler" for homosexuality in the American society. Furthermore, by portraying gay people in a positive light and homosexuality as normal, Hollywood is a "pusher" of homosexuality. Teenagers may be tempted to experiment with homosexuality as the direct result of the kind of movies that Hollywood produces.

Particularly in light of the punishment that the people of Sodom and Gomorrah received, Americans must feel alarm. What happened?

God committed genocide against the people of Sodom and Gomorrah, and it is seen as a righteous judgment of God.

This fact should give everyone pause in America. What does promiscuous support of homosexuality mean for America? The Biblical example shows that outcome can be quite tragic for everyone.

It is important to remember that God considers homosexuality as not only immoral but an unnatural act – going against the created order. Romans 1:22-27 states:

> *Although they claimed to be wise, they became fools and exchanged the glory of the immortal God for images made to look like mortal man and birds and animals and reptiles. Therefore God gave them over in the sinful desires of their hearts to sexual impurity for the degrading of their bodies with one another. They exchanged the truth of God for a lie,*

> *and worshipped and served created things rather than the Creator – who is forever praised. Amen. Because of this, God gave them over to shameful lusts. Even their women exchanged natural relations for unnatural ones. In the same way the men also abandoned natural relations with women and were inflamed with lust for one another. Men committed indecent acts with other men, and received in themselves the due penalty for their perversion.*

It is clear that God hates homosexuality. It is an abomination in God's eyes. And there is a sure judgement.

It is no surprise that often destroyed civilizations exhibit evidence of active support of homosexuality before their destruction. Greek society came to complete ruin as society leaders fell victim to supporting and propagating pro-homosexuality agenda in culture and literature. The Roman Empire fell as the royalty in that society unabashedly practiced homosexuality and encouraged homosexual practices in the society.

God has created human order in such a way that society cannot but fall when homosexuality is encouraged. This should not surprise anyone since Romans 1 is very, very clear.

The Bible clearly teaches that homosexuality is a sick and corrupt practice that will bring God's judgment. While homosexuality may be seen as the most advanced sinful form of sexuality gone bad, it is important to recognize that sexual purity as a generic theme is held up to be very important in the Bible.

Ephesians 5:3 commands: "But among you there must not be even a hint of sexual immorality, or of any kind of impurity, or of greed, because these are improper for God's holy people." The Word of God teaches us that we are to be holy as Christians because Christians are God's holy people. Being the people of God requires us to imitate the holiness of God.

Colossians 3:5 demands: "Put to death, therefore, whatever belongs to your earthly nature: sexual immorality, impurity, lust, evil desires and greed, which is idolatry." It is clear that God demands sexual purity. The list is dominated by a call to kill sexual impurity. The language is strong and clear.

1 Thessalonians 4:3-8 argues at length in order to persuade why sexual purity is important for Christians:

> *It is God's will that you should be sanctified: that you should avoid sexual immorality; that each of you should learn to control his own body in a way that is holy and honourable, not in passionate lust like the heathen, who do not know God; and that in this matter no one should wrong his brother or take advantage of him. The Lord will punish men for all*

> such sins, as we have already told you and warned you. For God did not call us to be impure, but to live a holy life. Therefore, he who rejects this instruction does not reject man but God, who gives you his Holy Spirit.

The Word of God is clear that it is God's will that Christians be pure. What God wants is for Christians to fight sexual urges that would lead to sexual sin and immorality. Not only should Christians control their own bodies, so as to guard against sexual sins, the Bible is clear in commanding that no Christian should take advantage of other Christians to commit sexual sins.

Concern for sexual purity of the Christian community is clear here. The Bible recognizes that there may be times when a Christian can be vulnerable (sexually) and that another supposed "Christian" can try to take advantage of her (or him). This Bible passage in 1 Thessalonians clearly warns against this.

Sexual purity is so important that God commands excommunication for gross sexual immorality. 1 Corinthians 5:1-5 requires:

> It is actually reported that there is sexual immorality among you, and of a kind that does not occur even among pagans: A man has his father's wife. And you are proud! Shouldn't you rather have been filled

> *with grief and have put out of your fellowship the man who did this? Even though I am not physically present, I am with you in spirit. And I have already passed judgment on the one who did this, just as if I were present. When you are assembled in the name of our Lord Jesus and I am with you in spirit, and the power of our Lord Jesus is present, hand this man over to Satan, so that the sinful nature may be destroyed and his spirit saved on the day of the Lord.*

The Word of God treats sexual immorality so seriously that it demands kicking out of church those who are rabidly sexually immoral. They cannot be given communion or allowed to participate in church life. This is very serious stuff. And the reason that the punishment is so severe is that God is very concerned with sexual purity. God demands sexual purity – on the individual level as well as on the corporal level.

The church must never practice sexual immorality or encourage it in its premises. Christians gathering together must think seriously about the need to gather in holiness and in sexual purity. God demands the purity of the church, the Body of Christ.

It is clear that sexual purity is very important to God. It is important to recognize that the emphasis on sexual purity includes abstaining from sex before marriage.

The Biblical demand for virginity before marriage is clear, especially in teaching regarding marriage. The Bible describes marriage as two people becoming one flesh. Of course, this is to be understood in a sexual way. When a man and a woman have sexual intercourse, they are being joined as if becoming one flesh. Ephesians 5:31 quotes Genesis in describing marriage: "For this reason a man will leave his father and mother and be united to his wife, and the two will become one flesh." The quote is from Genesis 2:24.

Genesis 2:24 is from the story of the Creation in the Book of Genesis. The verse is a part of the story of the creation of Eve. Genesis 2:21-22 describes: "So the LORD God caused the man to fall into a deep sleep; and while he was sleeping, he took one of the man's ribs and closed up the place with flesh. Then the LORD God made a woman from the rib he had taken out of the man, and he brought her to the man." The Genesis passage describes the woman being created and then explains why she was created. The creation of woman was for the sake of marriage.

Genesis 2:24 argues: "For this reason a man will leave his father and mother and be united to his wife, and they will become one flesh." Woman was created so that man can get married. In other words, Eve was created so that Adam can get married to her and "become one flesh."

It is important to recognize that marriage is a Creation mandate. In other words, God created marriage in the Creation before the Fall (through sin). Thus, we must understand that even if Adam and Eve did not sin, they would have been married. In fact, they were married before sin entered the world.

Why were they married? It is important to see the purpose of marriage. Genesis 1:27-28 gives us the explanation for why God created marriage (and man and woman):

> *So God created man in his own image, in the image of God he created him; male and female he created them. God blessed them and said to them, "Be fruitful and increase in number; fill the earth and subdue it. Rule over the fish of the sea and the birds of the air and over every living creature that moves on the ground."*

God created marriage so that man and woman would have many children. Procreation for the glory of God was the primary purpose of marriage. And in marriage a man and a woman become one flesh.

Can one flesh separate? Separating "one flesh" results in death. It is important to see that the physical union into "one flesh" was supposed to happen only in the context of marriage. The Genesis passage and its echo in the New Testament clearly show that sex should happen after marriage. It is only at the point of marriage that two shall become one flesh. Premarital sex is wrong. Two must not become one flesh before marriage.

The Biblical demand for sex – becoming one flesh – after marriage is a creation mandate. It is a law given at the Creation. The creation mandate precedes the 10 Commandments. And of course, we know that the 10 Commandments demands sexual purity and sexual intercourse only with your wife. Exodus 20:14 emphatically demands: "You shall not commit adultery." Adultery is having sex with someone who is not your wife (or husband). So having premarital sex is having sex with someone you are not married to. Thus, it is adultery (fornication is the technical term).

The Bible is clear about the value of virginity before marriage. Sexual purity is a value that is elevated over all other values in Christianity. The reason for this is clear. The marriage relationship is understood to be an early manifestation of the spiritual bond between Christ and His Church. Just as the church is consecrated by the bond in Christ, marriage is seen as a holy bond. It is not surprising, therefore, that weddings are often called Holy Matrimony.

What happens at marriage? God joins together a man and a woman in holy matrimony. A holy union occurs at the wedding. That is why ministers say: "Let what God has joined together, let not men separate!"

In a sense, staying virgins and avoiding premarital sex is a way of respecting God and His most important law for sexual purity. It is obeying the creation mandate and demand for Holy Matrimony.

The Bible is clear. Premarital sex is wrong.

For Yourself

For Yourself

Besides the instructions from the Word of God, the reason why you should not have premarital sex is that having it is hurting yourself. In other words, stay a virgin before marriage – for yourself – because not doing so will bring a bus-load of heart aches.

Let us understand why having premarital sex is hurting yourself. In order to understand the concept of hurt in relation to premarital sex, it is important to understand what sex is.

Of course, there is a crass way to talk about sex. So-called "locker room language" is not unfamiliar to most people who have gone through high school. But it's not confined to high school. Coarse conversation about sex exists at all levels of society and at every age group. Sometimes, flippant talk of sex makes it merely mechanical and not meaningful in any real way.

This is unfortunate because it gives a false picture of sex. Sex is meaningful. Maybe it is because there is so much meaning attached to sex that not-serious talk minimizes the worth of sex for everybody – especially for those who try to treat it not seriously.

It is important to realize human nature that is involved in flippant talk about sex. It may not be an exaggeration to say that men talk flippantly about sex to each other and that is a way they have come to bond on a base level with each other.

How does this explain the flippant talk about sex that often occurs between men and women? Men often talk about sex as if it's not anything serious because they desire to have sex. Men try to convince women that sex is not serious and it is not meaningful – that it is merely a superficial fun thing to do – so that they could get women to have sex with them.

For some reason – maybe by God's biological and psychological design – women instinctively treat sex more seriously. It may be attached to the reality of womanhood in which women have children. Sex leads to childbearing. This has been the case since the beginning of time. Because men do not need to bear the physical responsibility (and the psychological responsibility) of carrying a child inside for almost a year, they don't think about the seriousness of sex. It's a gender thing.

Furthermore, the fact that some men treat sex flippantly is a picture into the historical perception of women as "sexual objects." Men have often seen women as sexual objects who are there for their sexual gratification. The fact that they have needs – such as emotional and relational – often go ignored.

Because women are often perceived as sex objects, men often try to pigeonhole them into that cage. One of the ways they try to do this is by talking about sex as if it does not mean anything.

"It's just sex," some men would say. Incidentally, this is an excuse that is often readily verbalized when they are caught being unfaithful. Often, this excuse does not suffice. Women feel pain when their husband has sex with someone else. Sex is not just sex. Sex is not meaningless.

For Yourself

It is not only women who realize that sex is not just sex. Sex is meaningful. When men find that their wife is having sex with someone else, they are often devastated. If sex were just sex, then these men would not be upset in any way. It is because sex is so meaningful that people feel so much hurt when their loved one has sex with someone else.

Sex is meaningful. Sex is meaningful because it is not merely a physical act. Sex involves emotions and one's inner being. The seeming meaninglessness of sex that men and women often try to assert (or convince themselves of) in order to gratify their sinful needs results in personal devastation.

Human beings are emotional beings. Human beings feel. And human beings become attached. Even though a person may say or try to convince himself that sex has no bearing on his emotions. That's just not true. Sex bonds a person emotionally. This is true for the woman as it is for the man. There is an emotional connection. Sharing intimacy in such a close proximity cannot but bond people.

What kind of emotional damage can happen because of the sexual bond? There are many and I will name and discuss major pains in the realm of emotion caused by premarital sex.

The first major emotional damage is rejecttion. No one likes to be rejected. Guys know what kind of blow to personal pride it is when a girl rejects him for a date. And girls know how it feels to not have the guy you like ask you out. Those are "rejections" that bring emotional pain.

You can say what you will about this rejecttion, but surely for the person who experiences the rejection, it is very, very painful. For many, it may seem like the world is falling apart.

People try to minimize this pain, but often they do so because they are not you. If they were in your shoes, they would be feeling what you feel and they would not laugh it off.

Not only is it painful for you to experience rejection, however small it may appear to your friends, it is doubly painful every time you are reminded of the rejection.

The reason why you feel pain at rejection, as small as it may appear to your friends, is because you are an emotional being. You experience life emotionally. Every event that happens to you impacts your emotion. Thus, it is understandable why you would feel emotional trauma when the person you really like does not like you back or does not appear to like you back.

Even when it is "small" rejection, you feel pain. Now, think of "big" rejection. What would be a big rejection? Let's start with the girl? Let's say that you are the girl who has sex with some guy before you are married. As far as you are concerned, you have given him the most important part of yourself you can possibly give. There is nothing more physically you can give. And you are thinking that there is nothing more emotionally that you can give. You have shared your most intimate moment with him.

And let's suppose that he considered that a one night stand – a "conquest" – and never called you back after the sex. Or even if he sees you at work or at school, he ignores you after you have sex. How would you feel? You would be devastated beyond words. Why? Because you have experienced rejection. And this rejection is much more painful because you have given up what is so valuable to you personally. There is nothing more precious than your body. Nothing you own will ever mean more to you than the body you have. You can always buy a new car or replace your car with another. Your body is not like that.

So, when you give your body to someone, you have given him something that is most precious to you. You may not recognize this cognitively or consciously, but subconsciously as a human being you are programmed to protect your body as is the law of nature, so you instinctively understand (even if on an unconscious level) what you have given up. And the unconscious awareness impacts your conscious in ways that you may not comprehend. But it's very real. It's like when you are in love. You can't explain why you feel a certain way, but you are aware at some level that it is because you have feelings for this person. You may not even be sure why you feel this way – at first (even if you can cognitively understand it with time). Your psychological and emotional make up – what you are as a person – triggered something subconscious in you that impacted your conscious, so that you feel something. Sometimes, you can feel something so strongly that you feel your body hurt.

So, you can understand that such a process (the unconscious impacting the conscious) can be felt on other levels as well. And with sex, this is a strong element. Even if you try to brush it off and say that it was just a one night stand for you, too, you know that it isn't. There is something subconscious in you that impacts your conscious so that you become aware, even if against your own wishes. You feel emotionally. You understand. And when the guy leaves you after the one night stand, you know that you have experienced rejection.

It is not surprising, therefore, that when women become objects of one night stand, they often plunge into depression. Those who have seen their friend go through something like that have seen the mess your friend can fall into. You probably were shocked by how your friend, whom you knew for many years, started to act after she became the object of a one night stand. Maybe you were closer than a friend. Maybe it was your sister to whom the one night stand happened. Then, you may have seen the daily degeneration of the person whom you knew as your sister. She may take on a completely new dimension to her person, so much so that her personality becomes not recognizable. She may develop a type of guardedness that you never saw in her before – she may become mistrustful even of her closest relatives because of being the victim of a one night stand.

Here, we are talking about a girl who does not consciously understand what has happened to her. We are talking about someone who thinks that it was okay (or tries to convince herself that it was okay). Even someone who tries to convince herself otherwise, she realizes on an emotional level, even if not on a conscious level, that she has been a victim of rejection of the highest kind – that of her one and only body.

Now, consider what the effect will be on a girl who realizes that she has been a victim of a one night stand. You can well imagine that the effects will be compounded and the girl will become a mess. She may even become suicidal. Many girls, particularly in teenage years, who considered suicide did so because of a guy and it almost always involved sex and rejection.

The more intelligent the girl is the more she understands what the guy who had sex with her and abandoned her did to her. But it is not merely about book smarts. Sometimes, girls with book smarts are more "stupid" than those who don't even have a high school diploma when it comes to something like this. Why is this the case? The more education a girl has the more she is brain-washed by the secular educational system to think that sexual promiscuity is okay. The more she will think that it's normal. In a sense, the secular educational system has brainwashed her with their secular agenda. Thus, her God-given smarts and instincts have been dulled. So, it is logical that a girl without much brainwashing by secular academia may be more in tune with her instincts as a woman and in terms of emotional survival.

As much as I hate the theory of evolution, I would like to point out that even evolutionary scientists have pointed out that hunting and gathering was meant to procure a sexual partner. And according to this evolutionary tale, the man wants to have as many sexual partners as possible because he wants to procure descendants for himself. And according to them, they would say that the women are programmed by evolution to survive according to the evolutionary theory of survival of the fittest. Thus, she knows that she has to make sure that the guy doesn't have many sexual partners because that will mean her chances for survival will be minimized. Thus, she fights off other women who would want to be his sex partner because her biological instincts to survive kicks in.

Even the evolutionary scientists who do not have the Truth like us Christians acknowledge something that is true as found in the Bible. Why is this the case? Because there is general grace. God has given general grace to all creation, regardless of Christian and non-Christian. One of the things that is given in general grace is an understanding of truth relating to nature. This is spelled out in Romans 1. Of course, people taint the truth and evolution often does this. However, there are some points that support the teachings in the Bible and we can say that that's where they have not yet tainted the truth in nature as described in the Bible.

With the evolution story above, there are some points that these so-called scientists miss. They block out her emotional side. They describe things purely in terms of the survival of the fittest theory devoid of emotion. For the evolutionary scientists, it's all about instinct and not emotion. But we Christians know that God created human beings and we had emotion from very beginning. It is not an evolutionary development at a later stage of evolution of humans, like these scientists try to dupe us into thinking. Evolution is a theory and nothing more; it is not Truth.

The Bible clearly shows that God created human beings as emotional beings. Thus, it is understandable to see that emotionally God created humans – male and female. In other words, emotionally, God created humans to be monogamous. One man should marry one wife. This was the creation order. This is what God wants from people. This helps us to understand why Jesus Christ was so harsh in his teaching against divorce. Jesus Christ prohibited divorce and condemned the Mosaic Law for allowing divorce. Ideally, one man will marry one wife and they will be faithful to each other until the end. The guy should not run off with another girl because she's younger or more physically attracttive than his wife of 20 years. And vice versa.

God created human beings as emotional beings. And God created human beings to feel completion only with one person. Thus, two shall become one flesh. One plus one becomes one and not two. The Bible teaches the principle of marriage. Thus, sex is to be in the context of marriage. And true happiness sanctioned by God can be found in sex with one spouse.

Because this is the character of humanity instilled in every human being, any deviation from this brings about emotional trauma. Thus, when a guy has sex with a girl and leaves her after the one night stand, she feels devastation deep in her heart and she can feel pain all over in a real sense. Something against her created body has happened.

Something against what was meant to be happened. She may not fully comprehend every aspect of what has happened to her, but she will feel sadness and pain. And she will never forget this feeling until the day she dies – because she will remember.

Everyone feels the way God intended for human beings to feel. However, a person who receives much education may have been brainwashed to block out the natural feelings programmed into every human being. Our emotional make-up is impeded by secular education that seeks to go against what God intended for us to be. That is why a person with greater secular education may not be as in-tune with what we would biologically feel and emotionally feel. Thus, a girl who is more educated may try to brainwash herself whereas a girl with less secular education may be in tune with her biological and emotional make-up and its response to the breach of what was intended – for her to have sex only with one person.

Thus, it is not surprising to see that studies after studies show that girls who are less educated are often more guarded about having sexual promiscuity. However, a very educated girl is often sexually promiscuous because she has been brainwashed into subscribing to a secular system against the law order of God. But as much as the educated girl gives herself up to her secular brainwashing, that will not mitigate her feeling of pain and rejection. Education does not bring happiness. The educated woman will pain emotionally as much as the uneducated woman however she wants to philosophize her pain.

For Yourself

Those who have natural type of smarts – to understand what has happened to her – will feel greater pain, at least on a conscious level. However, in a sense, since the more educated will be prone to greater promiscuity because of her secular brainwashing, she may actually feel more pain in the long run.

Whereas a less educated girl may act our of her survival instincts and emotional make-up fairly intact and militate against sexual promiscuity for her emotional, psychological, and actual survival, the educated may ignore these factors in lieu of higher philosophy or some kind of literary fantasy. The educated often tend to be in less touch with reality than the uneducated, who live out reality on more practical levels.

For whoever understands on an emotional and self-awareness level what the one night stand represents, the pain will grow day by day. Rejection is difficult but when it involves your body, it leaves an indelible emotional mark. Furthermore, with each day, you can become more and more aware about the offense of the one night stand to your being.

You may think: How dare he make love to me and leave me like it didn't matter? You may feel a sense of hatred towards him. You may feel a sense of self-loathing. You may even blame yourself. There will be a myriad of emotions you will feel. The more aware you are the more you will feel pain.

One night stand can change a girl from a happy girl to a depressed and melancholy girl. Why?

Because she will feel that something very precious has been lost. She may think that it was stolen. She may think that she gave it up unwisely. But she will be aware that something precious to her that is an important part of her has left.

It is possible that such a feeling of depression and sadness can plunge her, against her genuinely true will, toward greater promiscuity. She may feel that maybe she is no longer worth anything. She has felt the big rejection, so she may think that she is worthless as a person. And a feeling of worthlessness may plunge her into a series of rash sexual experiences which she thinks irrationally will fill her emotional emptiness. Of course, they will not. In fact, they will plunge her further into emotional abyss and psychological turmoil. But as she is deep in her depression, she may not realize it. She may fool herself into thinking that she's enjoying them or they will make her feel better. They will only make her feel self-loathing in the long-run. She will snare herself into an emotional nightmare from which she would not be able to extricate herself.

Another possibility is that she may become more and more introvert. Contrary to popular belief, this is actually far better than the first possibility. Getting into sexual promiscuity kills the soul and waste away the person's dignity and self-respect. She will feel rejection after rejection – even if not on a cognitive level on subconscious and emotional levels, which are very real. The only way is down. Such a reaction may compel her into other problems

For Yourself

– such as substance abuse and other types of self-destructive actions.

When a girl draws inward and becomes more introvert, it is a natural defense mechanism and actually may help restore her to self-respect and dignity that she would need to be well in this life. Popular culture and secular psychologists often treat being introvert as something that is far worse. But this goes against Christian teachings. The Bible teaches that after great sin, you should become introvert. You should go away from the population and pray in fasting and in repentance. The Bible talks about putting on sackcloth and ashes (almost becoming social rejects by choice) so that those who have committed sin can have a time alone for contemplation and prayer. The Bible encourages *vita contemplativa* for the weary and the sick and the penitent. Becoming introvert is therefore a better reaction – it's a direction toward recovery. Of course, Christian leaders need to channel introvertsion toward introversion with repentance.

Secular psychology and worldly ideas of how to recover from depression or trauma are often wrong because they take God out of the equation. God created the world. The Bible contains an accurate picture of the human psyche and emotional make-up. How can those who purposely ignore the nature of humanity understand how to heal them? Of course, even dead clock is right twice a day, as the saying goes, and these secular psychologists may hit on something or stumble across a healing. But I would not bank too much on secular psychology and certainly popular media for answers.

Just think, secular psychologists are in a worse bind than you are if you are a true Christian. You are actually going to Heaven, whereas the secular psychologist is not. He has a greater problem in his hands than the greatest problem you can imagine for yourself.

The Bible is clear. God intended Adam to be with Eve. One man for one woman. Husband and wife to the end. Monogamous marriage is a Christian mandate. Thus, it is not surprising that a violation of this creation mandate will necessarily bring about pain, suffering, and trauma.

Even a single one night stand (or a violation of the creation mandate) will have emotional, psychological, and physical consequences. It is important to realize that not having premarital sex is important for your own sake.

Besides the pain and unhappiness you will feel because of the one night stand or pre-marital sex, your sexual promiscuity will cut your potential for greater happiness in future. If you marry a virgin, your sexual experiences will be that much more powerful and fulfilling than if you had multiple sexual partners before marriage. There are several reasons for this.

First of all, it will be special for you. You have decided to marry the love of your life with whom you will spend the rest of your life. Your first sex will be special to mark the beginning of your new life as the wife of the one you love, with whom you have become one.

Whether others know or not, it will be very special for you. You don't have to tell others how

For Yourself

special it is because it will be very special for you and you will know it. It's not easy in today's promiscuous culture to save yourself for marriage, and you have proven to yourself that you succeeded. You have won. You are not a loser when it comes to something that is so precious. And you have had this special, wonderful experience with the one you will spend the rest of your precious life with. The experience is special and you will emotionally realize how special it is.

The fact that it is your first time will be remembered by you until the day of your death. If you had sex before, you will have memory of the first sexual experience. You will have mixed up emotional feelings about that. You may feel a bit of emptiness inside because you did not give all you could to the man you love and have become one with – the one with whom you will live out the rest of your life. You will know in your heart that you could not give the most precious part of yourself because you have given it away. You cannot give away your virginity twice. You can only give away your virginity once. That is why it is the most precious gift that you can give the love of your life.

The knowledge that you have given your best, the most precious part of your life, to the man with whom you will spend the rest of your life will be a special thing for you, whether the man you are marrying realizes how special it is. You will know because as a woman you know how precious your virginity is and your first sexual experience.

Secondly, the first sex with your married partner will be fulfilling and special because you are giving yourself to him in fullness and full surrender. Every human being has a survival instinct and has doubts. There is no security in boyfriend-girlfriend relationship. You can break up any time. However, there is finality to marriage. Until death do us part, both of you will promise and confess. There is finality to the marriage bond, sealed in the Name of God the Father, God the Son, and God the Holy Spirit that gives you the security that you have been seeking for. As a Christian, you know that what is bound in the Name of the Holy Trinity is bound in Heaven as it is on earth.

Thus, when you give yourself in sex to your newly married husband for the first time, you will be giving yourself without any restrictions as is humanly possible. This kind of full-giving of yourself cannot be possible in a one night stand or a pre-marital sex relationship. Not only are there psychological and emotional factors that prevent the full-giving of yourself, there is the cognitive and epistemological process in your mind that confirms for you that you cannot give yourself fully to someone with whom you are not married. Your defense mechanism and survival instincts will be operating and will prevent you from enjoying the first sex in a meaningful and fully fulfilling way.

Besides the joy you derive from knowing that you gave your virginity to the married life partner and you have triumphed in preserving yourself and finding special meaning in giving the most precious gift you can (the only one you have and will ever have) to your half who makes you whole in marriage, you will also experience the pleasure

For Yourself

and true happiness of the experience in which you are giving yourself fully to your husband emotionally, psychologically, cognitively, and in every other way.

Furthermore, preserving your virginity until marriage and having your first sex with your husband will give you satisfaction and pleasure in the long-term because you know you have nothing to hide or feel guilty about.

If you had sex before, the husband will be curious about that. He will be wondering how he compares. He may even be fearful about whether he is able to satisfy you as well as someone else who had sex with you. As you know, fear breeds contempt. They say that even a mouse which is cornered by a big cat will attack the big cat. Because fear causes irrational behavior. Fear brings mistrust. Fear brings accusations. Fear creates barriers. Fear motivates decrease in love.

Thus, if the guy knows that you had sex with other men before marriage, he will start doubting himself and his ability to fully satisfy you. Even if you tell him a thousand times that he is the best and that he fully satisfies you, he will not believe you. It's only natural that he doesn't fully believe you.

Human beings are created with self-defense mechanism and it will kick in if you had sex with other men. Men are insecure beings to start with and the fact that you had sex with other men will make him that much more insecure.

What if the sex you have with your husband is not as physically satisfying? You have had your first sex with someone else and that was perhaps far more special than any sex you have with your husband from a psychological (woman) perspective because you lost what was most special to you. What are you going to tell your husband, with whom you will live the rest of your life with? You will be compelled to lie. You will have to hide your true feelings. You will have to hide your guilt.

To assume that your husband is stupid is a misjudgement. Most likely, he will be able to see through the deception and your guilt. Even if he doesn't tell you, he will feel it inside. You will feel guilty because you don't want to hide the truth from him. You don't want to feel guilty by lying to him. The guilt will give you misery. You would not have to worry about this guilt or misery had you preserved your virginity until the day of your marriage.

Besides the long-term unhappiness that can result from your sense of guilt and lies you have to tell your husband, you will feel miserable on other grounds as well. Because your husband is no fool – you would not marry a fool, would you? – he will see through your deception and lies. He will see through your guilt. And he will be able to see the truth behind it all.

And what do you think he will feel when he thinks that you had sex that was more special than those you had with him? He won't as a male be able to comprehend that the first time you had sex with someone will always be special for you because you lost your virginity to him. He is a man. His body is not built like you. He doesn't think like a woman. He thinks like a man. And so he will not be able to understand. Even the most understanding of men will have problem dealing with this.

What do you think will be further conesquences of this? He cannot help but love you less. Of course, he will tell you that he loves you just the same. But he will say that to make you feel better. He'll be lying to you the way you lied to him about your other sexual experiences. This is how men are built – they are very jealous and possessive. You can condemn your husband for being this way but men – all men – are like this. There is a reason why men have locker talk about sex as conquest. It's how men are built. For men to think that you have been "conquered" by another man is to attack his fundamental nature as a man – his masculinity comes under siege. The very knowledge makes him feel like less of a man. And there is nothing you can do to make him feel other wise.

Thus, even if you think about sex in completely other terms – because you are a woman – men think about sex in male terms. The very knowledge you had sex with other men will undermine his pure love for you and weaken the intensity of his love. It is only natural for men to feel this way. This is how men are created as men.

The Genesis account of the Creation supports this idea. God created Eve out of Adam because God wanted to teach the principle that the woman is to become integrally one with her husband. The wife must feel like she is physically linked in an integral, "one body" way with her husband. So, becoming one is not only on emotional or psychological levels in the Bible.

When the guy knows that you had sexual partners before marriage, he cannot control how he feels and how he is made as a man. He will necessarily love you less. Of course, even though he loves you less, he may love you more than any other woman alive. However, the intensity of his love (vis-à-vis you) will be weakened and there is nothing you can do to change that. He may lie to you but this is how men are built.

To illustrate this point further, think of you getting a 80 per cent on a physics exam. You got the highest score and 80 per cent is an A. However, you are thinking to yourself, you could have gotten a 100 if you did not make the stupid mistakes. You studied hard for your exam and you could have made 100. But you made those stupid mistakes. In a way, nobody's going to condemn you for getting an A with an 80 per cent. But you yourself know that you could have done better. You know that you could have gotten that 100.

It's like this. Your husband may love you 80 per cent and it's the "highest" intensity of love. But if you did not have sexual partners, your husband as a man could have loved you with 100 per cent. Women have to recognize that male pride is something that men cannot control themselves. It's part of the male physical and psychological make up from the days of Creation.

What does this mean for the woman? She is left with 80 per cent of his love and not 100 per cent because she had sex before marriage. So, having sex before marriage cuts into her satisfaction in life

For Yourself

and from experiencing 100 per cent of her husband's love.

This is what the Bible means when it tells us that sin has consequences. Even if we are forgiven for our sins, sins leave consequences. For instance, you can punch your brother in the face for no good reason. He gets a broken nose. You ask him to forgive you. He forgives you. However, that doesn't make his nose unbroken again. You will have to see your brother's broken nose for the rest of your life – his nose testifies against you. You are, of course, forgiven. However, certain things cannot be changed even if you are forgiven.

Such is the case of having sex before marriage. You lost your virginity, which you can only lose once in your lifetime. You can't unlose it. You can't lose your virginity again. That's impossible. Psychologically, you will remember that you have lost your virginity. The impact of having had sex before marriage will stay with you until you die. Of course, when you ask God to forgive you, He will forgive you. But that doesn't make you a virgin again. That doesn't take away the memories. That will not fail to leave an imprint on your husband. Sin is forgiven, but the consequences of sin will remain until you die.

Thus, your having sex with some guy before marriage adds to your unhappiness in the long-run – even if you have been forgiven by God and your husband tells you it's okay, you will experience the consequences of you having had sex before marriage.

Staying a virgin is a good idea not only because God demands it, but because it is a smart thing to do to procure your future happiness. Besides all the reasons why you should preserve your virginity until marriage, there is yet another reason why you should remain a virgin. Your preventing yourself from having sex before marriage will minimize you ending up in a divorce.

As mentioned, men are insecure beings. Your having sex before marriage compounds their insecurity. And men can act impulsively based on their insecurity. When men know that you had sex with someone else and realize that not everything you are telling him are factual, the man will not only start loving you less, he will start feeling inadequate. Thus, men will be more prone to look elsewhere.

If you had sex with someone else and he doesn't believe what you say about him is true, he in his male weakness may seek out women to confirm his masculinity. In his insecurity, he may want someone to reassure him that he is all that and more. He would not have had a need for this male weakness if you were a virgin when you married him. He would not have had to doubt at all in that department. The very fact that you had sex before marrying him tempts him in ways that are specifically male.

Obviously, if he is trying to assuage his male ego by seeking sex with other women, the likelihood is that your marriage will end up in divorce. So, you can see that it is not necessarily because he loves you less that he is cheating on you.

For Yourself

He may cheat on you to satisfy his male ego or assuage his male insecurity. Of course, despite the fact that this may be the fact in your husband's affair, it's not going to make you, as a woman, feel better. Furthermore, you will not be able to comprehend him, no matter how well he explains this male weakness. Because God created you female and you think like a woman and feel like a woman. That is why in the Bible, it says: God created them, male and female. God programmed males differently from females from the day of Creation.

But even if your husband does not actually have sex with another woman to satisfy his male weakness, your marriage can still fall apart if you had premarital sex. His doubts can irritate him and one day he will have a straw placed on his shoulder that breaks the camel's back. You won't see it coming because it will be aggregate, adding slowly through years and years.

What you will see is he becoming more and more emotionally distant. Like men, guys in insecurity and struggling with their sense of maleness will become detached. A woman may ask – why is her husband so detached? One explanation may be that you had premarital sex and his male insecurities from his knowledge and what he sees as your trying to cover up things will eat away at his affection and trust for you. Even if he doesn't recognize this himself as what is happening, things are happening on the subconscious level from the way he is programmed as a male.

You may not be able to identify the problem either. When your husband becomes emotionally detached, you may blame it on many other factors. But it is possible that you are totally wrong. It may all go to the fact that you had premarital sex.

Of course, he's not going to tell you that because it is humiliating for a man to tell his wife about his male insecurities based on the fact that his wife had sex with someone else. But it will eat away at him and this will be far more real to him than any peanut butter and jelly sandwich you make for your kids.

It is important to realize that the rate of divorce started to rise around the world after women had premarital sex. If you know societies where women are married virgins, the divorce rate is very low.

Of course, it is important to understand how men and women are built. It is important to recognize the reality of the male ego and male responses to their wife having had sex with other men. Often, modern psychology avoids this issue because psychology has often been anti-Christian and do not want to recognize Creation order and the reality of sin. But psychology does injustice to people who will experience divorce, if it ignores Biblical teaching about human nature and sin.

The best idea is to remain a virgin before marriage. It may seem like a difficult task but it will definitely be worth it for the sake of your long-term happiness. Instant gratification is not worth the life-time of heartaches. So, don't give in and have sex before marriage.

For Your Future Life Partner

Of course, you don't merely live for your own happiness but for the happiness of your husband with whom you will live the rest of your life. That is why it's important to talk about preserving your virginity for the sake of your future husband. You two will become one flesh.

Why is it important for you to remain a virgin for the sake of your future husband? Some of the reasons were discussed in the last chapter. Because your happiness in marriage is tied to his happiness in marriage as in marriage you two will become one, it is not surprising that some of the reasons why you should stay a virgin for yourself will coincide with the reason for why you should remain a virgin for your husband.

It is important to reiterate that being a virgin before marriage is the greatest gift that a girl can give to her future husband. This goes without saying. Since virginity is one thing that every woman has and it is the most precious thing she will ever possess – since she can only give it away once – it is understandable why it is the greatest gift that a woman can give to her husband.

Sometimes women do not realize this until it is too late. That is why God has established parents over a girl. The parents have a God-given obligation to ensure that she stays a virgin until she becomes an adult. The parents should protect her until she understands the value of her virginity and realizes what it means to give it away. The parents have a God-given duty to explain to her and help her understand why she must stay a virgin until marriage. A Christian parent who has failed to properly educate her daughter in this Biblical principle has failed as a Christian parent. No Christian parents can call themselves good Christian parents if they have not taught the importance of virginity to their daughter and reminded her time and time again. The relationship of the bride to her husband is likened in the Bible to the relationship between the church and Jesus Christ.

The reason that St. Paul makes this relationship is because he expects all Christian parents to teach their children not to have sex before meeting their husband. Just as the church should remain pure for Jesus Christ, the woman is to remain pure for her husband. St. Paul is over-concerned about sexual issues. In every Pauline epistle, you can see Paul's teaching on sex and against adultery.

We are not talking about the age of Hollywood. We are talking about the ancient world. Why did Paul preach so much about sex? Because preaching against sexual immorality is the Christian way. Today, you almost never hear Christian clergy preach against premarital sex regularly from the pulpit. You almost rarely hear Christian preachers talk against adultery from the pulpit. This shows how far the church has gone away from its roots. Preaching against fornication and adultery was important in the early church. Pauline epistles to various churches clearly show this.

A Christian church that is sexually impure has violated the body of Jesus Christ, which is the church. This is a grave wrong against God, which will result in God's destructive condemnation and judgement. God is not merciful to those who sin against the Body of Christ and refuse to repent. The church is a holy entity and its purity needs to be preserved. The New Testament's preferred language to talk about the purity of the church is one which describes a virgin bride who has kept herself pure for her husband. The church is the bride and Jesus Christ is the bridgegroom. Christians must not take this language in the Bible lightly.

The reason that the Bible emphasizes the virginity of Mary, who gave birth to baby Jesus, is for the same purpose. Sexual purity is a very important value in the Bible. Only a virgin body was worthy of carrying the incarnate Jesus in her womb. A woman who had sex would have disqualified herself naturally to carry holiness in her being. Mary was a virgin until the day she gave birth to baby Jesus.

The emphasis of the virginity of Mary in the New Testament should help us understand the New Testament church's overarching concern with women's virginity before marriage. To lose virginity before marriage in the New Testament church was seen as the greatest evil. One who lost virginity before marriage was seen to be a type of prostitute. Of course, prostitutes can become Christians through repentance, but the teaching in the New Testament clearly does not allow for being sexually active before marriage.

Those who are sexually active before marriage were seen as not holy individuals. Sex was the quickest route to losing holiness and being an enemy of God. St. Paul preaches most against sex and demands excommunication of those who persist in sexual immorality.

Today, Christian clergy are afraid to stand up for the principles of the Bible and teach as St. Paul did in the Bible. There are weak Christian pastors who allow sexual immorality to proliferate in the church. Such a pastor does not uphold the principles of the Bible. And that clergy will be under condemnation of God when Jesus Christ, our God, comes back in full glory in the Day of Judgment. Protecting the purity of the Body of Christ is the responsibility of the one who has been given the pulpit by God's grace and will. The Christian clergy must not fail our LORD Jesus Christ.

The Old Testament condemns the sexual immorality of the Israelites. If one reads the Book of Hosea, one sees the condemnation of adultery and fornication. It is for sexual impurity that God destroyed Israel. The most used language to condemn Israel was "prostitution." God condemns Israelites for prostituting themselves with Baal.

The imagery must be taken seriously. God was destroying Israel because Israel refused to be faithful to God. The idea that a community that believes in the Triune God of the Bible which cheats on the husband (the people of God are the bride and the Triune God is the husband) will be punished is seen as normal. Just like God demanded absolute faithfulness in "spiritual marriage," God demands absolute faithfulness of the wife to her husband in marriage.

Having sex with anyone who is not one's husband brings the anger of God. It is because the Bible emphasizes the need for faithfulness of people of the Triune God to the Triune God, that the Bible is overly concerned with sexual purity of the marriage bed. The marriage bed must not be tainted with sexual immorality. A wife who has sex with someone other than her husband violates the most sacred law of the Bible. There is a reason why the relationship between a woman and her husband in terms of faithfulness is used over and over again to describe the relationship between the Triune God and Christians (Old Testament's true believers were Christians as well because as the Bible teaches us, Abraham believed in Christ and was it was credited to him as righteousness, and "he was justified" – Those in the Old Testament who did not believe that Christ, God the Son, is God were not saved in the Old Testament; only those who believed in the Triune God of the Bible were saved in the Old Testament period as well as in the New Testament period).

A church which does not teach sexual purity in marriage does God a disservice. The church must preach regularly about sexual purity. The church must demand regularly that its young remain virgins until marriage. Guarding the virginity of the young of the church is one of the primary missions of the church. A church that fails to protect the virginity of its young members has failed in its mission as a church and must repent and reconstitute itself and its goals. This is clear from the Old Testament as well as from the New Testament teaching. No church can claim to be the holy body of Christ which allows its young to lose their virginity and does nothing about it. The church must protect the virginity of its young and if it does not then its integrity as the true church of Jesus Christ is in jeopardy.

To achieve this goal, the church must regularly teach its adult congregation the value of virginity in Christian faith – as St. Paul often does. Preaching against sexual immorality must be a regular feature of the teaching ministry of any church. Parents need to be taught to protect the virginity of their children. They have to be taught the Biblical principles, and the Christian leadership must give them directions on how to accomplish this in the context of the Christian family. The church must take an active stance against premarital sex.

The integrity of the relationship between the virginal church and Christ must be maintained. How will the analogy work if the church does not teach proper Biblical principle of the exclusive sexual relationship between wife and husband? The teaching that the church is the bride of Christ will not work. That is the reason why St. Paul preaches so much against sexual immorality in the local church context. In the Old Testament and the New Testament, believers of the Triune God are described as the bride of the Triune God. That is why there is an overarching principle for sexual purity in the Old Testament as well as in the New Testament.

Thus, the obligation to keep church's young to be virgins for marriage is a serious obligation of the local church. Church must work at preserving sexual purity like it does to work toward global missions. Paul preaches just as much about sexual purity (if not more) than he does about missions to the world. All Christian preachers must take a note of this.

Just as a church that fails to protect the virginity of its young has failed as a church, parents who fail to protect the virginity of their young have failed as parents. There has to be repentance, reconstitution of goals and directives, and execution of the Biblical principles to protect the virginity of the young.

Christian parents and Christian churches must fight to change laws that encourage premarital sex of the young. Since Christian churches and Christian parents are entrusted with the obligation of preserving the virginity of the young before they get married, they must change laws of the land so that they can accomplish their goals. Children spend five days out of seven in schools. If high schools become a place where sexual promiscuity is taught, then it becomes harder for the Christian church and Christian parents to accomplish their goals to keep their children virgins. If because of their school's influence, the children go out and have sex before marriage, still God will hold the parents and the church responsible. The parents must repent for being bad guardians of their children's Christian responsibility if they lose their virginity before marriage. It doesn't matter they were brainwashed by their public high school or not.

The parents are responsible as their guardians before the throne of Christ.

Christian parents often forget that they have an obligation before Christ. They have an obligation to bring up the children in the Word of Christ. They have an obligation to protect the virginity of their children until they get married. If the children marry non-virgins, the parents are responsible before God. The parents have sinned because they were bad Christian parents and did not fulfil their obligation to God as Christian parents.

There is a reason why the father gives the daughter away to the husband. This is based on the Biblical principle and the teaching of the Christian church about the responsibility to protect the virginity of the children before marriage. In essence, the father is assuring the husband that he has protected the daughter's virginity and he is giving her away to the husband as a pure, virginal bride. This is why the father gives the daughter away in the marriage ceremony and the daughter wears a white wedding dress.

In many countries, people have preserved the form of marriage ceremony but have forgotten the meaning behind it. One of the primary responsibilities of Christian parents is to protect the virginity of their children. If they have failed in this regard, they must repent before Christ. For Christ will hold them accountable at the day of Judgement for being bad Christian parents.

The bride marrying a virgin is the greatest gift that she can give to her husband. And Christian parents and Christian churches are obligated to uphold the Christian law to protect the virginity of the young. Not doing so is not only wronging Christ but it is also wronging the husband who is to marry the virginal daughter of the church.

As important as the responsibility of the Christian parents and the Christian church for preserving the sexual integrity of their children, preservation of virginity before marriage is the primary responsibility of the bride to be. It is important that you remain a virgin before marriage. You need to pray for strength from God. You need to pray that even in your weakness that God protect your virginity. You must pray for your virginity on a daily basis, and you must set time to think about ways to do this effectively. Staying a virgin is the greatest gift that you can give to your husband-to-be.

There are some suggestions on how you may accomplish your goal. First of all, it is important to avoid all temptation. Josh McDowell teaches that you should not French-kiss anyone because it can easily make you weak and lead to sex. Josh McDowell as America's leading teacher of teens knows what he is talking about. And most importantly, he is Biblical in his teaching. He agrees that preserving the virginity of Christian teens before marriage is a primary objective of the Christian church and a major obligation as a Christian. Don't put yourself in temptation by French-kissing someone. You may be weaker than you think.

Fundamentalist Christians have emphasized that you should not go to movie theatres because it can lead to sex. Many people used to laugh at

Fundamentalist Christians. But more and more, people are recognizing the wisdom of Fundamentalist Christians of the past. You go to the movies with a bunch of people, you may sit next to a guy, and he may put his arm around you. That could lead to something else and you may compromise yourself sexually. People are recognizing that this is not as far-fetched as it was once thought to be.

  Fundamentalist Christians of the past had one thing right for sure – you must avoid temptation for sex. Their emphasis that their children avoid movie theatres was a step toward protecting their children's virginity. To give you a modern day example, the Japanese government in one of its provinces made it illegal for young teenagers to go to movie theatre after 6 pm because they were afraid that this would lead to sex. Of course, they are not thinking in terms of Christian values – but they did not want promiscuity to taint their country. As Christians, how much more important it is for us to guard against sexual immorality because Christians have the Truth. Yet, a country that does not have the true religion is showing America the way. This shows how far America has gone down as a leader of morality since the days when Fundamentalist Christians were strong in America, several decades ago.

  Avoiding temptation is very important. Do not assume that you are going to be strong in the midst of temptation. You watch that X-rated movie, you may compromise your virtue. You go to a movie theatre on a date with just one guy, you may become weak and give in. You French-kiss a guy, you may end up losing your virginity because of your weakness. In prayer, think about what temptations to avoid so that you will not fall into committing crime against God by giving up your virginity before marriage.

Another way to protect yourself is to surround yourself with good Christian friends who also are concerned to preserve their virginity before marriage. You can tell a lot from the company you keep. If you hang out with people who don't think that losing virginity before marriage is a problem, most likely, you will lose your virginity before marriage. Daily conversations with your "friends" can wear your defenses down and even brainwash you in the long-run. Premarital sex is wrong. But if you keep non-Christian friends or so-called Christian friends who do not want to honor Christ with their virginity before marriage, you may cave in and commit the crime against Christ and have premarital sex.

Furthermore, you can protect yourself by waging a war on behalf of Christian principles. You can write to Hollywood and demand more Christian-friendly movies. You can write to *Seventeen* magazine and complain about overtly sexual content that would encourage girls to have sex before marriage. You can petition your public high school to allow Christian lecture for chastity and Christian values to be given public forum. You can write to your Congress Representative about passing legislation that favor Christian values. You can write letters to the editor in local newspaper criticizing articles that encourage a pro-premarital-sex position. You can write to pop music singers, particularly those known to be Christians, to promote virginity before marriage. There are many more things you can do pro-actively. And such pro-active stance against premarital sex before marriage will help keep your focus on the goal and mission to honor Christ with your virginity before marriage.

With God given mind, you can think of other ways to keep your chastity in tact before marriage. Since virginity is the greatest gift that you can give to your husband, it is important for you to focus on this. It is a precious gift.

Besides the fact that your virginity is the greatest gift that you can give to your husband, you should stay a virgin before marriage because your virginity can become a badge of honor for your husband.

Your husband will know that you have preserved the greatest gift that you will own in your life for him and him only. This is very special. He understands that. And the fact that you gave him your virginity will become a badge of honor for him. He will be able to have pride in this knowledge and in this fact.

You have to realize that marriage is a partnership. It's not just about you working to make the marriage a great marriage – it involves you and your husband. The two have to work together to make the one unit of marriage, sanctified in the Name of God the Father, God the Son, and God the Holy Spirit, one that is worthy of the holy union.

One way you can help your husband be zealous in making your marriage a complete success is by giving him the greatest trophy that you can – which, of course, is your virginity. You have saved yourself for the one person with whom you will spend the rest of your life with and when you are married you can give your virginity to your husband as his trophy of honor that will help him go through difficult temptations at work or in other social settings. Your husband is a man and has manly weaknesses. Of course, he should be strong in Christian faith to overcome all temptations, but he needs your help, too. Marriage is a teamwork. And Christ designed marriage as a teamwork that is to complement Christian faith.

That is why the Bible is so emphatic about sexual purity. If you remain a virgin for your husband and give your virginity to him as the greatest trophy that he could ever own, it will give him that much strength in human terms to be faithful to you and make the marriage work. There is a pay-off for you and your husband and your marriage for you to remain a virgin until you are married. Your life happiness may depend on it.

Any guy who's ever been to a locker room in high school knows that taking a woman's virginity is talked about in terms of trophy. Men know that once a woman's virginity is taken away, that's the only time she can "give it up." Men are human beings and just because men become Christians does not mean that they stop being humans or men. They will be men with all the frailty that accompanies that until they die. Keeping yourself a virgin before marriage is one strong help to ensure your life's happiness. For men, it matters a lot that they have been given that ultimate trophy by you. They don't want to feel like they were second choice. And certainly, if you gave away your virginity to someone else, obviously your husband is second best.

From a purely physical standpoint, this is true. It is true that you gave your virginity to someone else. In terms of your physical body, he is the best. Any guy who has sex with you after that is by definition, second best, because he is the second person to have sex with you. The guy can lie to you and tell you that it does not matter, but every guy knows that this matters. Men are designed that way – whether they are Christians or not is irrelevant. They will feel second best if you lost your virginity to someone else.

Think of giving up your virginity to someone else besides your husband as like the blessing of Isaac to Jacob. Isaac was supposed to bless Esau because Esau was the first-born. But Jacob tricked Isaac into blessing him. Jacob lied to his father by making his arms feel more hairy like Esau so that Isaac – being basically blind – would mistake Jacob for Esau and give him the blessing for the first-born. What made the whole situation unfair for Esau was that even Jacob's mother (who was also Esau's mother) colluded with Jacob to trick Isaac, her husband. And Isaac's wife also helped in the plot by making the stew herself for Jacob to give to Isaac to receive the blessing of the firstborn.

Isaac was truly tricked. Isaac actually thought and believed that it was Esau he was blessing. But, of course, it was Jacob in the disguise as Esau. However, this is the important fact to remember. Once Isaac gave away the blessing of the first born to Jacob, that was it. Isaac could not say: I recant! I change my mind! I am going to change my mind. Once the blessing of the first-born is uttered, it was transferred away and Isaac cannot retract it. It is like "spilled milk" to use an American idiom.

Esau came and told Isaac to give him the blessing of the first-born. Isaac responded by saying that he had already given the blessing of the first-born. Isaac told Esau that he cannot give him the blessing of the first-born. It was not in his power to change the prayer. God will listen to the prayer that has gone out. God will fulfil the blessing that Isaac has given to Jacob, even though Isaac was tricked into blessing Jacob. The blessing prayer would come true for Jacob.

Of course, we learn later that God would punish Jacob for tricking his father, Isaac. Jacob, too, is tricked in a major way. He worked years and years for the woman he loved and his own uncle exchanged the bride on the wedding night and gave Jacob the other daughter, whom Jacob did not love. Thus, Jacob was married and the marriage was sealed in God's Name. Jacob could not divorce her. So, Jacob had to work years and years more to marry the woman he loved – his uncle's other daughter. So, Jacob paid for his trick against his own father.

But the important fact remains, here. Once Isaac gave the blessing of the first-born to Jacob, that was that. Isaac did not have the authority to retract the blessing. Isaac did not have the authority to bless Esau with the blessing of the first-born. It was once in a life-time thing. It did not matter that Isaac was tricked by Jacob. It did not matter that Jacob's mother put him up to it. All that did not matter. The prayer would come true for Jacob.

The prayer of blessing for the first-born is a picture of the virginity that is to be preserved for the husband. Virginity can be given away only once. Once given away, it cannot be retracted. Virginity cannot be given away twice.

It does not matter if you were tricked into giving your virginity away by some rogue. It does not matter if you were put up to it by coersion, persuasion, and bribery. Once you give your virginity away, you cannot retract it. You cannot ever give your virginity away ever again to anybody else.

In the Korean culture, virginity is so important that the traditional Korean clothing for women was accompanied by a small dagger. In the Scottish culture, men wear a dagger with their traditional outfit. In the traditional Shikh clothing, men wear a dagger as well. For the Scottish and the Shikh, men's traditional outfits include daggers for fighting purposes.

In the Confucian Korean culture, men's traditional outfit does not have a dagger attached to them. But women's do. Why? Because a woman was expected to commit suicide if a man was about to rape her. Her body was seen as sacred so that if a

Korean woman was about to be raped, since she could not overpower the man and she probably could not win a dagger match with him, she was expected to kill herself with the dagger. The dagger's purpose was only to kill herself. She was taught from the age when she was old enough to wear the traditional outfit how she can effectively kill herself with the traditional dagger if she is about to be raped and there was no way out. Even a non-Christian Korean traditional culture valued virginity so much. How much more important is virginity to Christianity, which makes the Virgin Birth of Jesus Christ central to the Christian teaching on Justification by Faith and Propitiatory Atonement?

Yet, in America's Christianity, there is lack of respect for the value of virginity. Virginity is a central part of Christianity, not a secondary part. Christianity has so devalued virginity that Koreans often blame Christianity for promiscuity in Korea. It should not be this way. In the New Testament times, when Christianity spread, value of virginity spread to the annoyance of many Pagans, who resented the Christian emphasis on virginity. In fact, in certain countries, Christians were killed because their emphasis on sexual purity and holiness. America's Christian churches – by neglecting emphasis on holiness and sexual purity and virginity – has turned its back on the teachings of the Bible and Christian history of trying to glorify God through sexual purity.

Fundamentalist Christians are right – there needs to be refocusing on virginity as a value for Christians. Perhaps, Fundamentalist Christians complain correctly against Wheaton College's direction in allowing dancing in their university and permitting alcohol consumption by its faculty. Studies have absolutely proven that dancing increases the propensity for sexual downfall. And there is no one in America who will deny that alcohol provides greater opportunity for sexual sins. Fundamentalists may have a point in outlawing dancing and alcohol from their schools. Although theoretically, they may be done in godly ways, in practice, they almost never have been done in godly ways in the context of Christian history. Non-Fundamentalists would do well not to criticize Fundamentalist Christians for their effort to preserve virginity of their young and the holiness of the Christian church.

It may be important to remind ourselves what happened to poor Esau. Because the blessing of the first-born was given to Jacob, Esau was left with prayers of cursing by Isaac. It may not seem fair, but that's how it is.

Esau kept demanding from Isaac to give him the blessing of the first-born. Isaac said that he cannot give the blessing of the first-born because the blessing has been already given out and that it cannot be retracted. It is given out only once.

Esau complained and demanded that Isaac pray for him. Obviously, Isaac cannot pray the prayer of the blessing for the first-born because he's already prayed. He is forbidden to pray that prayer again. Praying it again would directly offend God and insult His Law. Besides, even if Isaac prayed the blessing in form in defiance of God's Law, God would not listen to him. It would be useless prayer even if uttered out-loud.

It's like when God told Jeremiah that he must not pray for Israelites. God had anointed King Nebuchadnezzar, the heathen king of Babylon, an unbelieving nation, to destroy Israel. So, any prayer that Jeremiah uttered for Israel, which was marked for destruction by God via the hand of God's anointed, King Nebuchadnezzar, would be in direct disobedience to the One True Living God. Of course, Jeremiah could have prayed for Israel and against King Nebuchadnezzar – against the explicit direction of the Triune God – and uttered the words out loud, but the fact is that the Triune God would not have listened to Jeremiah's prayer done in disobedience to Him. Jeremiah could only pray prayers of destruction for Israel. Since King Nebuchadnezzar was God's anointed to destroy Israel, any prayer regarding the situation by Jeremiah had to be prayers for King Nebuchadnezzar and the success of King Nebuchadnezzar's mission to destroy Israel, which was the will of the Triune God of the Bible against Israel.

Thus, it was the case with Isaac and Esau. Isaac could have uttered the blessing for the first-born again for Esau, but the Truine God of the Bible would not have listened to that prayer. It would have been a useless prayer. More importantly, it would have been deeply offensive to God who demanded the prayer of the blessing for the first-born be uttered out loud only once. Isaac, being wise, did not violate God's demand right before his death.

So, what did Isaac pray? Isaac prayed, in effect, a prayer of curses for Esau. Isaac prayed that Esau will serve Jacob for the rest of his life. Isaac prayed that Esau's descendants would serve Jacob's descendants. In effect, the prayer of cursing for Esau matched the prayer of blessing for Jacob. It did not matter that the prayer for Jacob was done because Isaac was tricked. The prayer was going to be fulfilled. And for the prayer to be fulfilled, Esau had to be necessarily cursed. That is the rule that God has set out, and Isaac dutifully obeyed the Triune God of the Bible.

Losing of virginity is like this. You can lose virginity by being tricked, by being sweet-talked, by being coerced, by all kinds of means. Once you lose virginity, you can never get it back.

What does this mean for your husband? Your husband is cursed with the knowledge that you had blessed someone else with your virginity. Whether he likes it or not, he has to live with the knowledge that he has been cursed as second-best – someone to whom the blessing of virginity was not given. Whether he tells you or not is irrelevant. You may seek reassurance from him because of your insecurity and he may be forced to lie to you and tell you that it doesn't matter to him, but the facts are facts. You have given your virginity away to someone else – and he will suffer mental torment. This is how God created man. The more you seek reassurances from him, the more you curse him and make him feel the curses upon his marriage because you have given your virginity away to someone else. Thus, your giving your virginity to someone else is, in effect, a curse of your marriage from the start. Sin has consequences.

If you wonder why there are so many divorces in the USA, you have your answer. The consequence of sin. The consequence of Christians losing virginity before marriage is that their marriage is cursed even before it begins. Some may survive through the curse that is brought on by loss of virginity before marriage but many don't. It is because you have lost your virginity before marriage that the chance you will be divorced and will not have marriage bliss for the rest of your life has increased. This is the way God has designed His universe.

Marriage of one man to one woman is a Creation Mandate. What this means is that even if Adam and Eve did not sin, marriage would have been between one man and one woman. The woman was to lose her virginity to one man and have only one sex partner until she dies. This was how the Creation was intended to be. Marriage was created before the fall of Adam and Eve to be between one man and one wife. This is clear in the Book of Genesis.

It is important to note that Jesus Christ upholds the Creation Mandate in His Teaching. Many Christians do not like to quote Jesus Christ's teaching on divorce. Jesus Christ absolutely forbids divorce. Many Protestants may be upset, but they have to recognize that allowing divorce goes against direct teaching of Jesus Christ. Jesus Christ does not allow divorce. In fact, Jesus Christ explicitly condemns the Mosaic Law which seems to allow divorce. Divorce was explicitly outlawed by Jesus Christ and is the most important teaching by Jesus Christ. There is no theologian – liberal or conservative – who denies that it is authentic teaching of Jesus Christ.

Thus, in forbidding divorce, the Roman Catholic Church is far more Biblical than any Protestant Church that allows divorce. Of course, Fundamentalist Christians forbid divorce and they are very Biblical as well. But there are a lot of wishy-washy Protestant churches that want to stroke the egos of the wealthy by pretending like divorce is okay. They do disservice to them and the Church of Jesus Christ. Jesus Christ's teaching against divorce is clear, like night and day. Divorce is forbidden. And certainly, those who are divorced are not allowed to marry again. When they remarry, they do so against the explicit direction of Jesus Christ in the Bible.

It is important to see that there would not be need for divorce if there was a better teaching on sexual purity. Most of divorces happen because of marital unfaithfulness. One sees why St. Paul constantly preached against sexual impurity – he was guarding Christians against divorce and encouraging holiness. Wife to husband is like the Church to Jesus Christ.

At the center of sexual purity and holiness, therefore, is the preservation of the virginity of the young. That is why the primary obligation (not secondary or tertiary) of Christian parents is to preserve the virginity of their children. The children in the church can lapse as Christians or walk away from the LORD. But they can always come back to the LORD. Once you lose virginity, you can never gain it back. It's irrelevant whether you go away from Christ for a time or whether you are a firm believer. Virginity, like the prayer of blessing for the first-born, is a once in a life-time thing. Its preservation is a symbol of the purity of the church. Your protecting your children's virginity will go a long way to ensuring their future happiness in marriage. So, the parental duty is not only on Christian, spiritual level, but on human parental level (to ensure children's happiness) as well.

The Christian church also must not think of preserving the virginity of church's young as a secondary or tertiary objective of the church. It is a primary objective. A Christian church can teach all the head knowledge it wants. If it fails to preserve the holiness of the children of God, it has failed. A church that fails to preserve the virginity of its young before marriage has failed as a church and that church must have a period of repentance before the Triune God and a refocus of the church's objectives before God.

That is why the Puritans had the "scarlet letter." The Puritans who were concerned with holiness developed a system to ensure sexual purity and virginity. Those who criticize the Puritans and their effort to preserve virginity of the young obviously tend to be those who have no problem with loss of virginity before marriage.

Thankfully, there are still Christian high schools in America which has as its primary objective preservation of sexual purity of their young. Although Christian colleges are going in a more lax direction these days, Bob Jones University in its heyday had been a model for other Christian colleges in going out of its way to ensure sexual purity of all its students. They dictated clothing styles and strict regulations regarding campus life to ensure the purity of the Christian church and the virginity of its students before they are married.

The destruction of the holiness of Christian Church in the loss of virginity of the young must be recognized by churches in America. Christ demands holiness of His church. The virginity of the young is a crucial part of it. Put another way, a church that has many of its young lose virginity cannot be said to be a holy church. It's important to understand the implication of such a crime against God as a church body. If the church is not holy, the grace of God will depart from that church. This is an important New Testament principle. That is why St. Paul has such a harsh instruction for sexual immorality in the Corinthian church. America's churches must treat the instructions in the Bible very, very seriously.

It is important to recognize that preponderance of divorce dishonors Christ. Jesus Christ gave few explicit instructions about daily life and relationships. Divorce is one such clear teaching about ordinary life. Jesus Christ explicitly forbids divorce. Jesus Christ does not say what jobs you can have and not have. But Jesus Christ explicitly said you must not get divorce and those who do get divorced must not remarry. This is the clearest teaching of Jesus Christ on any issue expounded in the Bible. It is something that cannot be explained away.

So, the Christian church must protect against divorce. One way to do this is to protect the virginity of the young. If they remain virgins as they are supposed to before marriage, then their marriage starts with the blessing that comes from the sexual union of one man to one woman in exclusivity. Divinely blessed union as intended will bring glory to Christ Jesus. Church that ensures the process of the covenant community of Christians will be less likely to see divorce fill the church. Divorce insults Jesus Christ because it is a direct attack on Jesus Christ's explicit orders to His followers. Thus, it is easy to see why protecting virginity of the young is a primary objective of the Christian church because it is integrally related to protecting the Christian church against divorce. Jesus Christ in the New Testament gave a holistic program to follow and many modern day churches are ignoring the explicit teaching of the Bible.

Marriage is a Creation Mandate. Marriage unites one man and one woman to become one. It is, therefore, a part of the Creation Mandate that you preserve your virginity for your husband. In fact, losing your virginity before marriage is far worse sin than killing a newborn baby by dropping her down a flight of stairs for no reason at all. Premarital sex violates not only the Ten Commandments, it violates the teachings of the New Testament. Not only that, losing virginity before marriage violates the Creation Mandate given before sin ever entered into the world.

For Christ's Church

Some may think that this chapter is redundant since Christ's Church was discussed at length in the last chapter. But it's not because everything is inter-related. Staying a virgin for your husband is a part of the covenantal relationship of the Christian church to the Triune God of the Bible. It is a part of fulfilling your personal covenantal obligations to the LORD Jesus Christ. It is a part of keeping the Christian Church pure. It is a part of parents' duty to Christ – to whom you belong.

In this chapter, we will focus in greater depth about your personal obligation to Christ's Church. We will discuss a lot of related topics to why your staying virgin for Christ's church is important. In the discussion, you will better understand your place in the Christian Church, in the plan of God for your life, and in the world in Christian terms.

Best place to begin this discussion is with an explanation of the nature of the Church. What is church? Simply put, church is the body of Christ. Body of Christ is made up of believers of Christ, who have been baptized in the Name of the Holy Trinity – God the Father, God the Son, and God the Holy Spirit.

St. Augustine has a good explanation on the nature of the Church. St. Augustine distinguishes between the visible church and the invisible church. The visible church is made up of all those who confess Jesus Christ as LORD and are baptized. The invisible church is made up of true believers of Christ, who will spend eternity in Heaven.

There is certainly an explicit understanding that not all who belong to the visible church belong to the invisible church. People can see the members of the visible church, but only God can see who the members of the invisible church are. Ultimately, what matters for eternal life and salvation is not your membership in the visible church, where you have the approval of humans, but your membership in the invisible church, whose membership is recorded in the Book of Life that God owns.

Thus, it is possible for you to be a member of the visible church and go to eternal damnation in Hell. This is just as true for someone who goes to a liberal church as much as those who go to conservative churches. What you see is not what you get. St. Augustine recognizes that it is possible to fool the visible church, but it is impossible to fool God.

It is possible that you have been baptized, but you are not truly saved. It is possible that you stood in front of the church and gave your tear-jerking testimony about how Christ changed your life and still go to Hell. Only God knows who is going to Heaven or not. It's possible that you are genuinely misled by false teaching and accept Jesus as a nice person and think that you are going to Heaven. Of course, with all good intentions, you are going to Hell because you do not recognize the divinity of Christ. If you don't believe that Jesus Christ is God, then you are going to Hell.

Good intentions do not get you into Heaven. You have heard the saying, "Road to Hell is paved with good intentions." Where do you think this saying comes from?

For Christ's Church

You can be a member of the visible church – even a very good Bible-believing visible church – and still go to Hell. What insures your entry into Heaven is true regeneration in Jesus Christ. Who will judge this? Jesus Christ Himself at the Day of Judgment.

We have to take the warning of Deuteronomy 29:29 seriously. Secret things belong to the LORD our God, but things revealed belong to us and our children forever. And the revealed Truth can only be learned from the Bible.

From the Bible, we do know how we may be saved. We are saved when we accept Jesus Christ as God, who took on human body to die for us on the cross. Fully as God and fully as man, Jesus Christ died for us on the cross. Then, Jesus Christ rose from the dead and sits on the right hand of God the Father. We have to believe in the Holy Trinity – God is in Three Persons – God the Father, God the Son, and God the Holy Spirit. We have to believe that salvation can come only through Jesus Christ and no other redeemer.

If you do not believe in these things, you will go to Hell. This is clear from the Bible. So, if you think Jesus Christ is a nice person, you will go to Hell. If you believe that it's possible to be saved apart from Jesus Christ, you will go to Hell. If you think that there is no Holy Trinity, you will go to Hell. If you don't believe that Jesus Christ rose from the dead, you will go to Hell. If you don't believe that Jesus Christ is God, then you will go to Hell.

These are simple truths that are certain. If you don't believe these things then you can be 100 per cent certain that you are going to Hell.

Let's say you say to me that you believe in all these things. You can still go to Hell. Why? Because you can be lying to me. You may not believe in all these things but may just say that you believe them. I may not be able to see through you, but God can. And He knows you are lying and you do not believe in all these things. So, you will go to Hell.

How about if you genuinely believe in all these things? You still can go to Hell if you are not justified from your sins. Only God knows if you are truly justified. In fact, only God can justify you.

What are possible scenarios where you may not be truly justified even if you believe all the "simple truths" mentioned above? For instance, your faith may not be a complete faith. You may believe but not with conviction of the heart and certainty – you are wavering between faith and lack of faith about all of the points above. In such a case, it is more than possible that you are not truly justified. How can you be when you have not put your complete faith in Christ?

True regeneration is followed by deep coniction that can lead you to death because your faith will make you choose death over life when your Christian faith is involved. If you fear the power of the secular sword and betray Jesus Christ and the Kingdom of Christ (like Judas Iscariot did), it is a good sign that you are not truly justified. Maybe

For Christ's Church

you thought you were. Maybe others believed you were. But in reality, you weren't.

The lessons from Judas Iscariot must be learned carefully. We are talking about one of the 12 apostles. We are not talking about just a simple follower of Christ. We are not talking about one of Jesus' close disciples. We are talking about a Billy Graham of Jesus Christ's generation. In fact, unlike Billy Graham and others since the ascension of Jesus Christ, Judas Iscariot was trained by Jesus Christ Himself! How many people can say that? Judas could. Even Billy Graham cannot say that he's an apostle. Judas Iscariot was an apostle!

Even though Judas Iscariot worked with Jesus Christ in holy work of God and in missions, he was not justified. He was not truly saved even though he was one of the 12 apostles! Hell was reserved for him. No one saw through him. Only Jesus Christ did. That is why Jesus Christ said at the Last Supper that the one who dips his hand will betray Jesus Christ.

It is important to remember that Judas Iscariot performed miracles like other apostles. Judas Iscariot drove out demons in Christ's name. Judas Iscariot did all the things that 12 apostles did. Still he was not a born-again Christian. He was not justified. He went directly to Hell when he died.

This teaches us that you can be working for the church all your life and still go to Hell. Judas Iscariot was administered the LORD's Supper by Jesus Christ Himself – and he still went to Hell. Mass will not guarantee your place in Heaven. You cannot buy your way into Heaven.

Only God knows who belongs in the invisible church. Certainly, Judas Iscariot, one of the 12 apostles, did not. Of course, it should not be surrising to see your elder, deacon, or even the pastor in Hell. If Judas Iscariot can go to Hell and he was one of the 12 apostles, your senior pastor can certainly go to Hell. Only God knows who is in the invisible church.

St. Augustine's teaching on the visible church and the invisible church has become the foundation of Christian understanding of the church for over 2,000 years. John Calvin and Martin Luher strongly agreed with this teaching – it has solid support from the Bible, of course.

Thus, when we talk about the Body of Christ, we must keep the distinction between the visible church and the invisible church in mind. The Church is the Body of Christ. What we see is the visible church. We see the visible Body of Christ. But the true Body of Christ is not the visible church that we see, it is the invisible church that only the Holy Trinity can see.

What this means is that when we talk about protecting the Body of Christ, we are NOT talking about protecting church members. It is possible that 90 per cent of church members in an evangelical church will go to Hell because they are not truly born-again. Only God knows.

So, when we talk about protecting the Body of Christ, we are not talking about church members, at all. For all we know, 90 per cent of them are not part of the true Body of Christ. They have no claim to Heaven. Since we have no way of knowing who belongs to the Body of Christ (ie, the invisible church), we never talk about church members when we talk about protecting the Body of Christ.

When we talk about protecting the Body of Christ, we talk about the requirements found in the Bible for protecting what Christ wants of the church. In other words, we talk about the Ideal Church.

It is important to understand what this means. We are not talking about church members. We are not talking about protecting the senior pasor because he can be a Judas Iscariot. Only God knows his heart. We are not talking about deacons and elders because they are human beings and are corruptible. They can even stand against the Body of Christ, while serving as deacons and elders in a "church."

We never refer to people and church memers when we talk about protecting the Body of Christ. Never ever! Even if all the members in your church are killed by a hurricane, that's okay. The Body of Christ is intact.

The Body of Christ refers to the invisible church – all those who are truly saved in God's eyes around the world. So, even if all the "Christians" in America died from a nuclear holocaust, that's okay. The Body of Christ is in tact. Christ's Kingdom is not of this world. True believers who died in the nuclear holocaust are in heaven. Besides, there are Christians in Indonesia who are part of the Body of Christ on earth.

When we talk about protecting the Body of Christ on earth, we are, therefore, talking about protecting the Ideal Church – what the Christian church should be. Thus, what we mean is protecting the correct teaching of the Bible. Thus, if an Episcopalian church down the street is installing a homosexual as the senior pastor, protecting the Body of Christ may involve killing him before he is installed to the position of senior pastor. Body of Christ is the Ideal Church which is supposed to be pure.

As you can see, protecting the Body of Christ may actually involve killing a person wearing the cloak of the clergy. Judas Iscariot was 1 of the 12 apostles. If he did not kill himself, the other apostles would have had to kill him. Thus, one must never talk about protecting the Body of Christ as protecting church members or even Chrisian ministers. The Body of Christ is the invisible church, which no one has access to. Secret things belong to the LORD our God. But revealed things belong to us and our children. We know that homoexuals must not be installed as a senior pastor of any Christian church. Protecting the purity of the Body of Christ necessarily involves blocking such an installation at any church – it doesn't matter whether you are Episcopalian or Baptist, there is only One Body of Christ in the world.

It was to protect the Body of Christ that the first thing John Calvin did after the Reformation and founding of the city of Geneva was to kill those who were threats to the Body of Christ – the Ideal Church as outlined in the Bible. John Calvin recogized that protecting the Body of Christ was not protecting church members. In fact, many of those killed were so-called Christians.

Martin Luther and John Knox did the same after the Reformation. In order to protect the Body of Christ, they killed so-called Christians who posed a threat to the Ideal Church as outlined in the Bible.

Killing of homosexual ministers before they are installed as senior pastors would be in line with protecting the body of Christ. In the same way, if a person in the church is pushing homosexual rights in the church and refuses to leave, then the church members have the God-given right to kill him. It is not only legitimate but obligatory that you find a way to kill this person so that the Body of Christ is protected. In other words, not killing a homosexual pastor would be sin and crime against God. Protecing the Body of Christ is not about protecting physical lives of baptized people on earth, it is about proecting the Ideal Church as outlined in the Holy Scriptures.

Letting pro-homosexuality lobby groups exist in a church is tantamount to desecrating the Body of Christ. If they refuse to leave, then Chrisian Law dictates that they be killed in some way. Preservation of the purity of the Body of Christ is crucial.

It is important to understand what the Body of Christ is in light of the Biblical teaching on the visible church and the invisible church. Christ clearly taught us this. Jesus Christ said that not everyone who calls Jesus Christ LORD (Greek word for the Hebrew word "Yahweh") will go to Heaven. What this means is that even those who call Jesus Christ God will not go to Heaven. (In fact, most Hindus call Jesus Christ "God.")

Jesus Christ also taught that even those who may drive out demons in the Name of Jesus Christ will go to Hell. It is because he does not belong to the invisible church – he is not truly saved in God's eyes. Jesus Christ said not everyone who performs miracles in the Name of Jesus Christ will go to Heaven. Again, you can perform miracles in Christ's name but in God's eyes, you may not be truly saved. You are not a member of the invisible church. Christ is clear on the distinction between the visible church and the invisible church.

One of the signs of a true Christian is being zealous to protect the purity of the Body of Christ. If you are willing to kill the homosexual clergy who is being installed as the senior pastor in the Episcopalian Church down the street, you are probably a genuine Christian, and a member of the Body of Christ (the invisible church). If there is a homosexual being installed as a senior pastor in the Episcopalian church down the street and you "don't give a damn," then there is a high likelihood that you are not truly saved and you are really not part of the true Body of Christ (the invisible church). You have fooled yourself into thinking that you were truly saved. Many people do. Not all who call on Jesus as LORD will go to Heaven. Your baptism, your personal testimony before the church, your work for the church may be only visible indicators and certainly will not secure your place in the Kingdom of Christ.

Obviously, installing a homosexual to a position of a senior pastor of any church is a great offense to the Holy Trinity and is an extreme case that demands immediate action. But the principle to uphold the purity of the Body of Christ must be evident in all concerns of the Christian church.

    Fundamentalist Christians in America in 1920s best showed what that meant. Fundamentalist Christians outlawed drinking and forced the change of US law to forbid drinking, for instance. The question is not whether drinking is sin or not. What's important to learn from that is the zeal of the Fundamentalist Christians to defend the Body of Christ. Sometimes, they took things a little bit too far. But it's better to be on the safe side than be sorry.

    Allowing homosexuals to be a senior pastor of any church brings down the condemnation and judgment of God on all Christians of the land. Thus, every Christian in America is liable for God's divine judgment on the USA if there is even one openly homosexual clergy in the position of senior pastor anywhere in the 50 states. It doesn't matter what your denomination is or if his denomination is different from yours.

    This principle is important and explains why African and Asian Christians fought homosexual ordination so strongly within the Episcopalian denominational structure. That is the right attitude in trying to keep the purity of the Body of Christ.

    Where does your virginity fit in? If you are concerned to preserve your virginity before marriage, then there is high likelihood you belong to the invisible church, the true Body of Christ. If you have no concern to preserve your virginity before marriage, you probably do not belong to the invisible church, even though you may fool yourself into thinking that you belong to the invisible church. God determines who belongs to the invisible church, not you or any other human being.

If you do not feel in your heart any desire to remain a virgin before marriage then you should re-examine your salvation. You probably are not truly born again. You probably do not have the Holy Spirit residing in your heart to give you Christian conscience and conviction to protect the Body of Christ. You are probably going to Hell when you die.

The most visible sign that you belong to the Body of Christ is the zeal to protect the Body of Christ. If you don't have this zeal, most likely you do not belong to the body of Christ.

Preserving your own virginity is integral to the demands of Christ to preserve the purity of the Body of Christ. As a human being, you can fall into sin. But if you don't feel at all guilty about giving up your virginity or if you are really ready to give up your virginity and your conscience is clear, you certainly do not have a Christian conscience. Barring any special divine revelation, you must abide by the principles of the Holy Bible.

The Bible makes clear that God does not provide exceptions, except in some cases with prophets. Prophet Hosea was to violate Biblical Law and marry a prostitute because God commanded him. This did not mean that others could do such a thing. God demanded this only of Hosea for prophetic purposes. Anyone who violated this Biblical Law would have been held accountable in ways that Hosea was not because he was directly commanded by God.

Elijah and Elisha both broke Biblical Law as prophets because God commanded them to on various occasions. Again, there were specific orders from God to show prophetic enactment of why God was angry with Israel and how God was going to punish Israel. For prophetic message of judgment and for prophetic enactment alone were they specifically allowed to break Biblical Law as stated in the Bible. Their breaking of Biblical Law on God's order did not mean that others were allowed to follow their example. Barring any direct divine directive, Biblical Law holds tantamount for everyone. Barring any special divine directive, willful violation will certainly bring down divine wrath and judgment of the most horrific kind.

The principles of the Bible must be upheld at all cost. The Body of Christ must be protected even if it means waging a Christian Holy War and giving up our lives. Many Christians have died because they stood up for the honor of Christ Jesus and the sanctity of the Body of Christ.

It is in this spirit that you must treat protecting your virginity, which Christians throughout history have described as protecting your Christian virtue. If you give up your virginity, you give up your virtue in the eyes of God. It is a serious offense.

You have to remember that your marriage to your husband is likened to the relationship of the church to Jesus Christ. You must not forget that.

You can see how you can go to church all your life and go to Hell. It's possible that 90 per cent of the members of a typical evangelical Christian church are not saved. Where's the proof? Homosexual clergy gets installed down the street at a Congregationalist Church, how many churches care? Certainly, this is a proof that most of the members of that church are not truly saved – or they would care about protecting the Body of Christ.

It is important to heed the words of Jesus Christ. Jesus Christ taught us that if we want to be His disciples, we must (1) deny ourselves, (2) take up our cross, and (3) follow Christ. Deny ourselves of what? It can be our freedom because we choose to kill the openly gay clergy who is about to be installed as the senior pastor of the Congregationalist Church down the street. Take up our cross? What is the cross but the instrument of death? Maybe you may not plan it well and you are arrested for first degree murder of killing the openly gay clergy. You get the death penalty by a state that refuse to uphold God's law against homosexuality. You don't die a sinner in the eyes of God. You have upheld God's law. You should be willing to suffer the death penalty which is your cross in following Christ. Discipleship involves personal sacrifice – even one's life. Jesus Christ made that clear in His teaching. The truly saved will take Jesus Christ's call to discipleship seriously.

The principle is the same in regards to protecting your Christian virtue before marriage and staying a virgin. You must deny yourself, take up your cross, and follow Jesus Christ. You must deny yourself of the premarital sex. You must be willing to die for your virginity. And you must follow Christ. Your virginity is very important to your Christian faith. St. Paul does not teach at length about sexual purity and establish Biblical principles of sexual purity for no reason. It is integral and foundational to the Christian faith.

It is important to understand that if you are a true Christian, you belong to the invisible church. As a member of the invisible church, you have an obligation to protect the purity of the Body of Christ (which is the invisible church). If you have no concern to protect the purity of the Body of Christ, then certainly you are not a part of the Body of Christ (the invisible church). It's one sure way to know that you are not truly saved – if you have no concern to protect the purity of the Body of Christ.

What does this mean in the wider context? Not only should you be concerned about your virginity, you should be concerned about the virginity of every other Christian around you. Your obligation to the Christian church in terms of virginity and the purity of the Body of Christ is to encourage your Christian friends not to have sex before marriage. You must convince them not to have sex before marriage. You have to persuade them not to have sex before marriage. If they are in heat, then lock them up in your room and guard them if you have to so that they will not go and have sex and lose their virginity.

You have an obligation not only to yourself but to your Christian friends to guard their virginity. Positive peer-pressure may help protect the purity of the Christian church. Most studies show that teenagers consult their friends before having sex with their boyfriends or someone else. If the Christian friend whom they consulted stood their ground and strongly protested, many would not have gone through with the pre-marital sex. Often, it is the permissive attitude of the friends or even tacit encouragement of friends, which leads to sex before marriage.

You have to make your position very clear even if you may lose your friend. Sex before marriage is wrong. Pre-marital sex corrupts the Body of Christ. Your friend may be weak because she thinks she has fallen in love. Christian brothers and sisters are there to be strong when one of the church members becomes weak. That's what Christian love is all about. Christian love is about being there to stop your friend from falling away from Christ. Christian love is stopping your friend from having pre-marital sex.

You may not love her enough to discourage her not to have pre-marital sex. You may not love her enough in Christ to overcome your fear of alienation as the result of leading your friend toward path to life – spiritual life. You have to learn to love with the love of Christ – which is self-denial. Just because you want her affection as a friend, if you selfishly not warn her, then obviously, you have not practiced Christian love.

Christian love is not like world's love. You can be a nice person to someone – that's world's definition of love and friendship. Christian definition of love and friendship is mutually encouraging each other toward Christian living. That is Christian love. There is a difference between Christian understanding of friendship and love and worldly understanding of what a nice friend is.

Preserving virginity before marriage has to be a group effort. Satanic forces are too strong and try to snatch up Christian virtue. Hollywood's movies seem to encourage "giving it up." Public schools in the USA are highly anti-Christian and encourage pre-marital sex. Even teachers encourage it. It is not easy to prevent pre-marital sex.

In such a difficult situation, it is important that Christians show each other Christian love and support. Christians should encourage and pressure each other towards holiness at all cost. Christians have to exert positive peer-pressure.

You should preserve your virginity for Christ's Church and you should help your friends to keep their virginity for the Body of Christ as well.

Conclusion

Conclusion

There are many reasons why you should not have pre-marital sex. Pre-marital sex can hurt you consciously and unconsciously and impact your psyche for the long run. Pre-marital sex can hurt your future marriage because of the baggage it will bring. Pre-marital sex can sabotage the happiness and longevity of your future marriage.

Staying a virgin can be a trophy to yourself in showing how you overcame despite pressure and difficulties. Virginity can be the greatest gift that you can give to someone whom you have successfully chosen as your husband, with whom you will spend the rest of your life.

As noble as these reasons may be, the most important reason that you should stay a virgin before marriage is because that's what the Bible teaches you should do. It is in humble obedience to the Word of God that you can experience true happiness that touches both your heart and soul.

Besides, keeping your virginity in tact before marriage is your duty and obligation as a member of the Body of Christ. Of course, if you have no desire or wish to keep your virginity before marriage, you are not truly born again. Maybe you can forget it all and just go to Hell and suffer eternally in excruciating pain forever. That's your choice, of course. God gives you a choice. But I wouldn't recommend Hell. In fact, I wouldn't wish it upon my worst enemy.

Hell exists. And the majority of the world will go there. It would not be surprising to see even 90 per cent of a Bible-believing evangelical church ending up in Hell. Bible clearly states that only a few will go to Heaven; not many.

It's up to you, of course, if you want to go to Heaven and live eternally in joy with Jesus Christ or if you want to go to Hell after experiencing worldly pleasures and suffer eternally for it in the Hellfire.

If you choose to go toe Heaven, then you have to be truly born again. And only God will know if you are truly born again.

If you are born again, then you will belong to the invisible church. And belonging to the invisible church has obligations. One of the most important obligations is to keep your virginity before marriage. This is an important role you can play to preserve the purity of the Body of Christ on earth.

Hopefully, you will not fail.

About The Author

Sam Goode is a popular evangelist who specializes in teaching teenage Christians values of historic Christianity. He has extensive theological training in the USA and in Europe and teaches young people around the world.

www.ingramcontent.com/pod-product-compliance
Lightning Source LLC
Chambersburg PA
CBHW020915090426
42736CB00008B/644